AF378423

# Rail Scene
## in colour

# Rail Scene
# in colour

Compiled by **Robert Antell**

LONDON
**IAN ALLAN LTD**

'Now, lads, you will live to see the day when mail-coaches will go by railway, and when it will be cheaper for a working man to travel on a railway than to walk on foot.'
*George Stephenson*

First published 1978

ISBN 0 7110 0873 6



Design by R. Antell



Published by Ian Allan Ltd, Shepperton, Surrey, and printed in the United Kingdom by Ian Allan Printing Ltd

*Title page:* A special from Stranraer to Glasgow approaches Glenwhilly station headed by HR 4-6-0 No 103 and GNSR 4-4-0 No 49 in April 1963. / *D. Cross*

# Introduction

Colour photography came too late to record in detail the zenith of steam in the 1930s, but thanks to the preservation movement the liveries of those and earlier years have been seen again on Return to Steam specials and on the preserved lines. The railway enthusiast has always been keenly alive to colour. Mention any part of the United Kingdom and somewhere in his mental picture of it there will be a gleam of Midland red, Brighton yellow, Great Western green and so on. In these days of standard Rail Blue there is less variety, but the train and its environment can still combine to make memorable pictures.

The views presented in this album are selected from among the many fine colour studies which have appeared in other Ian Allan publications (*Railway World, Modern Railways, Trains Illustrated* and *Locomotives Illustrated*). They have been brought together to illustrate a number of themes. 'Steam finale' takes us back to the 1960s when the steam locomotive was soldiering on to provide the backbone of the railway service while the problems of introducing and maintaining new forms of motive power built under the Modernisation Plan of 1955 were being smoothed out. The condition of the engines in those days was rarely glamorous but there were some interesting varieties of livery among the rolling stock.

'British rail rover' looks at diesel and electric motive power in service on many parts of the BR system. In the 1960s some would have refused to believe that affection would be felt for the earlier products of the Modernisation Plan when obsolescence overtook them. A correspondent to an Ian Allan magazine once complained that a diesel was visible in a picture of a steam train and requested the Editor to make sure that it did not happen again. There has been a notable change of attitudes since then. The diesel railcar may seem an unlikely object for nostalgia, but there is something very appealing about the single unit pausing at Sandplace on the Liskeard to Looe line to pick up a solitary passenger which appears on page 51. The Beeching Plan pruned many of the remoter sideshoots of British Railways but where they remain they are still a part of rural life.

At the opposite pole to the rural branch is the main line served by HSTs. The album gives a glimpse of what BR publicity has aptly described as 'the changing shape of Rail'. As the HSTs spread, the number of locomotive-hauled passenger trains will decline, although luggage space in the units is limited and locomotive-and-coaches formations will still be necessary on services scheduled to carry parcels and mails among others.

The final sections show something of the preserved lines, both narrow- and standard-gauge. Preservation has kept some historic lines in action with their original equipment, and has provided havens where a surprising variety of BR, Grouping, and even pre-Grouping locomotives can recreate the atmosphere of the steam age. *Rail Scene in Colour* blends the pleasure of the steam railway with the excitement and anticipation of the present time when new routes are being opened up to Inter-City 125 service and the electric APT is on the way.

**Steam Finale**

At the end of the second world war one of the most urgent questions affecting the future of railways in Britain was the type of motive power to be used. Diesel traction had made big strides in North America, and important main-line electrification projects were to be put in hand on the Continent. In Britain, however, the diesel locomotive had only become established for shunting duties, although the LMSR and the Southern Railway both initiated experiments after the war with main-line diesel traction, and the Great Western was investigating the gas turbine. Some 15 years earlier the Weir Committee had recommended general main-line electrification in Britain. Even if economic conditions had made it possible to contemplate such an undertaking in the post-war austerity years, there was still the immediate problem of keeping traffic moving.

In 1948 the railways were nationalised. British Railways took over some 20,000 locomotives of 448 different types which reflected the practice of the previous railway Groups and the individual ideas of their chief mechanical engineers. While steam continued it would be necessary to streamline the situation in order to economise in spare parts and set up a unified maintenance organisation and procedure for the whole of the BR system. A first step was to decide which of the existing locomotive classes might be adopted as standards for future building for express passenger, freight and mixed traffic working. The Locomotive

Exchange trials of 1948 were undertaken for this purpose, but although they produced much valuable technical information they did not show up any designs of obvious superiority to their rivals. It was therefore decided to produce a new series of standard designs incorporating the best features of those which had gone before.

A former Chief Mechanical & Electrical Engineer of British Railways has recorded that he spent his youth near a steam locomotive depot and what he saw of the work and conditions did not encourage him to enter the railway industry. He chose electrical engineering, and that was the route by which he came back to railways in the end. It was already being recognised before the war that traditional railway workshops and motive power depots compared unfavourably with contemporary factories as places of work and that this caused recruitment problems. Various steps were taken to improve matters. The LMS undertook a system-wide programme of mpd modernisation in which layouts were improved and new equipment was introduced to ease the more arduous and dirty jobs. At the same period all the railways made detail changes in design which enabled locomotives to run longer without attention, thereby improving operating economy and relieving some of the burden on the depot staff. One device was the self-cleaning smokebox, in which wire mesh screens broke down the larger cinders drawn into the smokebox from the fire so that they were small enough to be ejected through the chimney while the locomotive was working. The accumulation of ash in the smokebox was much reduced and clearing by shovelling was only necessary when the engine came in for a boiler washout. Some progress was made before the war with the fitting of rocking grates in which the firebars could be oscillated to disturb the ash so that it fell into the ashpan instead of remaining on the bars to form clinker. More might have been done in this direction had it not been for the excellent quality of steam coal available to the railways at that period. The practice was followed with more energy after the war when coal quality became very variable.

Another development in post-war locomotive building was the wider use of roller bearings. Hot boxes became less frequent and locomotives could run longer between repairs. Advantage was also taken of developments in metallurgy. Fitting maganese steel liners instead of white metal faces to the coupled axlebox slides of Stanier 'Black 5' 4-6-0s increased the mileage between repairs by 30%.

After the Exchange Trials of 1948 had been studied and assessed, the standard designs adopted for new locomotive construction aimed at combining maximum simplicity and accessibility with optimum steam raising. Most of them were required to undertake mixed traffic work. Self-cleaning smokeboxes, rocking grates, and ashpans with hopper doors for easy emptying were fitted to all designs. All were two-cylinder locomotives, with outside cylinders to meet the accessibility requirement and at the same time save the cost and maintenance involved in a built-up crank axle for a drive from an inside cylinder.

Six standard designs were put in hand at first: the Class 7 and Class 6 Pacifics, and Class 5 and Class 4 4-6-0s, all of which were mixed traffic engines. The other two were passenger tanks, the Class 4 2-6-4T and the Class 3 2-6-2T. Class 7 is best remembered as the 'Britannia' Pacific. There were some early mechanical troubles after the first 'Britannias' came out in 1951 but they soon settled down to prove themselves excellent engines over the range of duties for which they were intended, fulfilling their designers' aims of good steaming capability and low maintenance. Class 6 was a lighter version with smaller grate area and heating surface, and a boiler pressure of 225lb/in$^2$ as against 250lb/in$^2$ in the 'Britannias'. They were named after Scottish Clans. The two 4-6-0 classes were based on LMS practice, Class 5 being derived from the LMS 'Black Five' and Class 4 being a

6

lighter version of the same basic engine. LMS influence was seen again in the Class 4 2-6-4T but the Class 3 2-6-2T was based on the GWR 45XX class of the same wheel arrangement.

In 1953-4 three more standard designs came out — three small 2-6-0s of Classes 4, 3 and 2 and a Class 2 2-6-2T. The Class 4 2-6-0 proved a versatile engine and showed a useful turn of speed on cross-country passenger services. The last BR standard class appeared in 1954 — the Class 9F 2-10-0. Surprisingly with this wheel arrangement, the engine was intended for mixed traffic as well as heavy freight work and was given coupled wheels of 5ft dia. The wartime 'Austerity' 2-10-0s, the first British engines with this wheel arrangement, had 4ft 8½in wheels. Class 9F soon showed that it was fully capable of passenger train speeds when necessary. Two cases are on record of 9Fs reaching 90mph, one of them on the 'Flying Scotsman'.

The last of the BR steam designs can hardly be described as 'standard' since only one locomotive was built. This was the Class 8 Pacific No 71000, *Duke of Gloucester.* Unlike its forerunners it was specifically an express passenger design, but by the time it emerged in 1954 the British Transport Commission's Modernisation Plan was on the eve of publication and among its objectives would be 'fast, clean, regular and frequent services, electric and diesel . . .'.

The standard classes worked side by side with the 'classics' of the Grouping period and the rebuilds and new construction of the war years and after. On the LMR, 'Jubilees', 'Black Fives' and Pacifics looked much as they did in the pre-war years, but rebuilding of the 'Royal Scots' with Stanier taper boilers had begun in 1943, based on the 4-6-0 *British Legion* of 1935 which had used the chassis of the high-pressure 'Scot' *Fury,* destroyed by a boiler explosion. The East Coast main line exhibited a medley of Pacifics; there were the traditional Gresley engines which under the LNER had been Classes A1 and A3, and the Thompson and Peppercorn variants. Swarming somewhat in the manner of 'Black Fives' on the West Coast neighbour were Thompson's B1 mixed traffic 4-6-0s. The streamlined A4s rolled superbly on and came into their own again as the return to post-war normality brought the requirement of more frequent, faster but lighter trains. They

*Below:* BR 'Britannia' class Pacific No 70013 *Oliver Cromwell,* the last 'Britannia' to remain in service with BR, is seen with a special train commemorating the centenary of the completion of the Midland main line into St Pancras passing through Chesterfield in June 1968. / *Brian Stephenson*

continued to work non-stop London-Edinburgh services when these were restored and accelerated, and were more economical on coal than the Thompson and Peppercorn types with their larger fireboxes designed for high rates of steam production on the very heavy trains of the war years.

Bulleid's 'Merchant Navy' and light Pacifics were introduced on the Southern in 1941 and 1945 respectively. In later rebuilding the former lost both the streamlined casing that had earned the first of them the name of 'Spam cans' and the unorthodox Bulleid valve gear; some of the lighter engines were treated similarly. In their new guise both classes were held in much esteem by enthusiasts. An unrebuilt 'West Country' is credited with the highest drawbar horsepower recorded during the Locomotive Exchange trials of 1948 — 2,010dbhp at 67.8mph.

The Great Western Railway introduced a new locomotive class in 1945. During the war years there had been talk of a Pacific with 280lb/in$^2$ boiler pressure as a successor to the 'Kings'. Work on a new express passenger locomotive could not be undertaken during the war but when the construction of new mixed traffic 4-6-0s was authorised near the end of hostilities the 280lb/in$^2$ pressure and 6ft 3in driving wheels which were to have been features of the Pacific were adopted by F. W. Hawksworth in his 'County' class. The 'Kings' and 'Castles' continued their traditionally fine performances after nationalisation. In their later years double chimneys and blastpipes were fitted to all the 'Kings' and certain 'Castles', improving the power output of both.

Of the occasional departures from conventional steam locomotive design in the last years of steam, Bulleid's 'Leader' was the least orthodox. It was carried on two six-wheel bogies, each driven by a three-cylinder steam engine with sleeve valves. There was a driving cab at each end of the boiler and a central cab for the fireman. After limited trial running the project was abandoned. Another experiment was the fitting of ten Class 9F standard freight locomotives with Crosti boilers. In this arrangement, developed in Italy, feedwater passes through a drum underneath  the boiler proper where it is heated by the gases from the fire. Exhaust steam from the cylinders is led back through pipes to a blast chamber towards the rear of the boiler. The gases are drawn through the drum into the chamber by the vacuum created as in a normal smokebox and escape with the steam to atmosphere through a chimney on the running plate in front of the firebox. The chimney on the smokebox is used only while lighting up the fire, the orifice being closed by a hinged cover when the engine is running.

When the Modernisation Plan was launched it had been estimated that steam still had a life of 20 years on British Railways, but in 1960 the announcement that Class 9F 2-10-0 No 92220, *Evening Star,* on its emergence from Swindon, was the last steam locomotive to be built had an ominous ring. Meanwhile some steps had been taken to preserve noteworthy locomotives of earlier years. When ex-Glasgow & South Western 4-4-0 No 62777, *Gordon Highlander,* was withdrawn in 1958 the Scottish Region had it repainted in GSWR colours and used it together with ex-Caledonian single No 123 on enthusiasts' excursions. Later ex-NBR 4-4-0 No 256, *Glen Douglas,* was similarly restored for working specials, sharing this work with the pioneer Highland Railway 4-6-0 No 103. The 'Caley' single and Highland 4-6-0 had been preserved on their withdrawal before the war but at that time were simply static exhibits. South of the Border the Southern Region in 1962 gave T9 4-4-0 No 120, the last British survivor of that wheel arrangement, a new lease of life in London & South Western colours for excursion purposes.

Withdrawals of steam locomotives accelerated in 1962. On 16 June 1963 A4 Pacific No 60008, *Dwight D. Eisenhower,* worked the last scheduled steam train out of Kings Cross and all East Coast expresses were diesel-hauled south of Peterborough. A year later it was the turn of Paddington, which saw its last steam train on 11 June with the departure of the 16.15 to Banbury behind No 7029, *Clun Castle.* Also in 1964, with electrification into Euston proceeding apace, steam was banned on the LMR south of Crewe and steam locomotives which might have ventured to intrude were marked with a yellow diagonal band on the cab sides as a reminder that they were not to be allotted to duties that would take them into forbidden territory.

Electric trains began working into Euston in November 1965, although the official takeover by electricity did not take effect until the following year. By that time Waterloo was the only London terminus with a main line steam service still in operation, the Bournemouth/Weymouth trains continuing steam-hauled until the Bournemouth electrification was completed in 1967. The last day of steam at the terminus was 8 July 1967 and the last steam-hauled passenger departure was a boat train to Southampton Docks at 18.20 headed by rebuilt West Country Pacific No 34037, *Clovelly.* Steam had become extinct in Scotland a few weeks earlier.

In the North, however, the summer of 1967 still saw the last LMR Jubilees active on the Saturdays 06.40 Birmingham-Glasgow between Leeds and Carlisle. The North Eastern Region by this time was using steam only on freight services but these could still show the vintage spectacle of Q6 0-8-0s and J27 0-6-0s at work. By the beginning of 1968 only the LMR had steam in service on a few trains in the North-West. The official 'last day of steam on BR' came on 11 August 1968 with an excursion from Liverpool Lime Street to Carlisle and back. It seemed that the experience of travelling behind a steam locomotive on a BR main line had gone for ever. Yet in 1972 No 6000 *King George V* steamed triumphantly up to London with the Bulmers Cider train and launched the era of Return to Steam excursions which with BR approval and eventual participation have brought many giants and veterans of the steam age back to active service.

**Modern Motive Power**

Before the modernisation Plan for British Railways was launched in 1955 an energetic start had been made on replacing many steam-hauled local services with trains formed of diesel railcars and trailers. Publication of the plan revealed a more drastic programme which included 'the complete replacement of steam as a form of motive power by diesel and electric traction'. On the electrification side the Plan gave high priority to completing the Southern Region's electrification to the Kent Coast, which had reached as far east as Gillingham before the war. It also proposed electrification of the main lines from Kings Cross to York, and from Euston to Manchester and Liverpool. Such major works as these could clearly not be completed for some years and in the meantime improved main-line long-distance services would be provided by diesel traction.

In 1955 only a handful of diesel locomotives was in service. Under the Plan initial orders were placed for 174 locomotives from various builders, all resources available being called upon so that the changeover from steam could begin as early as possible. A diesel engine cannot be geared directly to the wheels of a locomotive like an electric motor but must drive through a system with similar functions to the clutch and gearbox of a motorcar. In most of the diesel multiple-units the engines were coupled to a change-speed gearbox by a fluid flywheel which took up the drive automatically as the driver accelerated the engine. He then changed gear with a manual control at certain speeds.

The fluid flywheel and gearbox system is less suitable for the high power diesel engines in locomotives and for these electric or hydraulic transmissions are used. All BR diesel locomotives today have electric transmission but hydraulic systems were in use on the Western Region until the withdrawal of the last of the 'Western' class in 1977. The decision to standardise electric transmission had been taken earlier after enough operating experience of both systems had been obtained for a comparison of their suitability for BR requirements to be made.

In an electrical transmission the diesel engine is coupled to a generator which supplies electrical power, equivalent to the mechanical power produced at the engine crankshaft, to electric motors geared to the axles. No gearbox is necessary with this arrangement. With the engine running at a speed selected by the driver, the speed of the train varies according to load and gradient in such a way that the power from the engine is always fully absorbed but not overloaded. The transmission behaves as if it were a continuously variable automatic gearbox.

In Germany successful results had been obtained with hydraulic transmissions in which torque-converters produced an effect similar to that of the electric system. The Western Region was made the proving ground for diesel-hydraulic traction and equipped its diesel locomotives with Voith or Mekydro systems of German origin. A torque-converter needs a high-speed drive and so the WR diesel-hydraulic classes were powered by engines running at around 1,500rpm. For a given power output a high-speed engine such as this is lighter than one operating in the medium-speed range of about 750-850rpm, and the overall weight of the diesel-hydraulics was significantly less than that of most of the diesel-electric classes of the same period. There was strong backing for the diesel-hydraulic principle, but the high-speed engines needed more frequent maintenance and a single hydraulic transmission could not handle more than about 2,000hp. The WR 'Warships' and 'Westerns' were of 2,200hp and 2,700hp respectively and were powered by two engines, each driving the axles of one bogie through its own transmission. The most powerful single-engined diesel-hydraulic locomotives were the 'Hymeks' with a 1,700hp engine and one transmission system.

The first of the diesel-electrics to appear were the 1,000hp mixed traffic units of the present Class 20, soon followed by Classes 31 and 40. The 2,000hp engine in the last-named belonged to a 'family' which began in the pioneer LMS diesel-electrics Nos 10000 and 10001 and has its latest descendant in the 3,250hp freight diesel-electrics

of Class 56 introduced in 1976. Today, although set to give 3,250hp in BR service, the engine has a rating of 3,520hp at 900rpm.

Although high-speed diesel engines were at first mainly associated with diesel-hydraulic traction there was an important exception in the prototype 'Deltic' locomotive. This was not in the modernisation programme but was a private venture by the English Electric Company to show that a 3,300hp diesel-electric for express passenger traffic could be built with a weight as low as 100 tons. It had two 1,500rpm engines rated at 1,650hp, each driving a generator supplying power to three of the six traction motors. The engines were of a design originally developed for high-speed marine craft and worked on the two-stroke cycle. With few and not notably successful exceptions, other engines in British diesel locomotives and multiple-unit trains have

been four-strokes but the 'Deltic' amply bore out its designers' hopes. A series of 22 (Class 55) was built for the Eastern Region and has worked the fastest expresses on the East Coast Main Line since 1961. The prototype 'Deltic' is now preserved in the Science Museum in London.

The most powerful locomotives in the Modernisation Plan diesel orders were the 2,300hp 'Peaks' (Class 44), increased to 2,500hp in later construction (Classes 45 and 46). All these classes were powered by Sulzer engines with two banks of six vertical cylinders each driving a separate crankshaft. A step-up gearbox combined the drives to give a higher speed at the output shaft to which the generator was coupled. When the requirement for higher power arose, it was provided by an engine of the same type rated at 2,750hp. This is the power unit installed in the very numerous locomotives of Class 47.

Up to and including Class 47, all BR diesel-electric locomotives had been equipped with direct-current traction generators. As powers moved up towards 3,000hp the limit at which these machines can be satisfactorily used was approached. In the 3,250hp Class 56 the engine drives an alternator, and the alternating current output is converted to direct current by silicon rectifiers. There is, in fact, a kind of rectifier in a direct-current generator — the commutator — but

this is in effect a quick-acting mechanical reversing switch which can give trouble when the power demand is high. Alternator/rectifier systems are likely to be used in new diesel-electric construction throughout the power range.

While developing its range of engines for rail traction, the English Electric Company produced a 2,700hp unit which was built into a prototype locomotive, 'DP2'. After experience gained in trial running the engine was installed in the Class 50 locomotives introduced in 1967 to provide accelerated services on the Crewe-Glasgow section of the West Coast Main Line pending electrification. They were transferred to the Western Region when the London-Glasgow electrification was completed. This class was notable for extensive use of electronics in the control system, setting a pattern for future development.

Now the way ahead for high-speed diesel passenger services has been pointed by the High Speed Trains. The fast-running diesel engine is back, for the Valentas in the HST power cars produce their 2,250hp at 1,500rpm and drive alternators similar in principle to those of Class 56. The vital function of supplying electric power as high volts at low amperage or vice versa, according to demand, no longer depends on servo-driven arms sweeping over contacts but is performed electronically. The power units also provide supplies for air-conditioning, lighting and catering services in the train, functions not originally catered for in most of the main-line diesel locomotives although many have been equipped similarly in recent years. Perhaps the most obvious forerunners of the HST were the 'Blue Pullmans' which ran in the London Midland and Western Regions but we should not forget the resourcefulness of the Scottish Region in taking existing locomotives and rolling stock and forming them into push-pull sets with a locomotive at each end for a fast Edinburgh-Glasgow service. A railwayman has aptly described them as 'Do-it-yourself HSTs'.

Electric traction on British Railways made a sharp change of course in the 1950s. The Liverpool Street-Shenfield and Manchester-Sheffield-Wath electrifications, completed in 1949 and 1954 respectively, had been planned before the second world war. They used the 1,500V direct current system which had been recommended in two pre-war reports and their motive power was based on established practice. When main-line electrification out of Euston and Kings Cross was proposed in the Modernisation Plan, it was at first assumed that these schemes would also be with direct current at 1,500V.

In 1930 the Weir Report had recommended widespread main-line electrification to take advantage of the country-wide availability of industrial electric power from the Grid distribution system. At that time it was accepted that the power, distributed as alternating current, would have to be converted to direct current for use in the trains, and there were important developments in rectifiers for this purpose. Many railways in other parts of the world used alternating current for traction, but they could not take it direct from their distribution systems because the standard industrial frequencies of 50 or 60Hz were too high for the traction motors. They therefore either generated their own supplies at only a half or a third of the standard frequency, or installed converting machinery.

Shortly before the second world war the German Reichsbahn had experimented on a line in the Black Forest with several types of locomotives that could work direct from a 50Hz supply, either by the use of motors specially designed for that frequency or by collecting the current from the contact wire at 50Hz and converting it into direct current on board. After 1945 this part of Germany was in the French zone of occupation and French engineers decided to carry on with the work. By 1952 they had equipped a line of their own in the Savoy and were ready to hold an international conference at which French, German and Swiss engineers demonstrated the progress that had been made. The *Journées d'Information d'Annecy*, as they were called, were the starting point of rapid development in the use of industrial frequency current for railway traction, and a system which at first had been proposed as a low-cost means of electrifying secondary or branch lines was soon to be applied on such important main routes as Paris to Strasbourg and Paris to Lille, and on the cross-country link from Dunkerque to Basle with its traffic of heavy steel trains as well as international passenger services.

With this system of electrification the contact wire is energised at 25,000V (usually written 25kV) and the current collected by the pantograph is led through a high-speed circuit-breaker to a transformer, where the voltage is reduced to a level suitable for the traction motors. In some locomotives at first the low voltage supply passed from the transformer directly to the traction motors, which were of special designs to accept the 50Hz frequency, but it soon became the general practice to install rectifiers which converted the output from the transformer into direct current, and to power the locomotives with direct current motors. The high voltage enables the points at which the contact wire is supplied with power to be widely spaced, and sites can be chosen where the railway and a Grid power line are close to each other so that little extra cabling is necessary. The feeder stations are simpler than the lineside substations of direct current railways, consisting only of transformers and protective switchgear. The transformers are necessary because the voltage of the Grid lines may be in the range of several hundred thousand volts and has to be reduced to 25kV for the railway supply. The contact wire system itself is the only link between the feeder stations. No interconnection by lineside power cables such as are used between substations on a direct current railway is required.

These developments were closely watched by British Railways engineers and when a report on future electrification in Great Britain was published in 1951 it was recommended that a small-scale experiment with 50Hz electrification should be undertaken here. The lines chosen were those of the former Midland Railway between Lancaster, Morecambe and Heysham, already electrified on the older alternating current system at 16 2/3Hz. Electric working on the new frequency began in 1953 with existing multiple-unit stock which had been equipped with rectifiers and new dc motors.

There was no suggestion in the Modernisation Plan of a change to the new system for the proposed LMR and ER electrifications, but only a year after the Plan was published it was announced that future main-line electrification outside the Southern Region would be at 25kV, 50Hz, and that the 1,500V dc sections from Liverpool Street to Shenfield and Southend Victoria, which had already been electrified, would be converted to the new system.

The first projects undertaken under the new programme were from Manchester and Liverpool to Euston; the Glasgow suburban lines north of the Clyde; Liverpool Street to Hertford East, Enfield Town, Chingford and Bishops Stortford; and Fenchurch Street to Southend. Orders were placed for 100 locomotives of five types (the present Classes 81 to 85) and 361 multiple-unit sets, the latter being the largest fleet of 25kV emus built up to that time. Another characteristic of all this first generation equipment was that it was designed to run on 25kV or 6.6kV, the lower voltage being used on certain sections where clearances between the overhead lines and other structures were restricted. The dual-voltage arrangement was used on the Eastern Region and in Glasgow, but by the time the LMR scheme began going into service experience had shown that lower clearances could be allowed safely and no low-voltage sections were necessary.

The locomotives differed in various aspects of their electrical equipment but all were of the Bo-Bo wheel arrangement and weighed around 80tons, with ratings in the 3,000hp range. All were equipped with rectifiers and dc motors for by this time it was apparent that the future lay in this direction rather than with special alternating current machines. Some designs both of locomotives and motorcoaches had mercury-arc rectifiers based on industrial types but adapted to prevent splashing of the mercury pool with the vibration of the vehicle, which could lead to 'backfires' and a shut-down of power. But the age of the semiconductor rectifier had already begun. The devices which had made the transistor radio possible were now being produced in sizes capable of handling high power; rectifier equipments with germanium and silicon diodes were included in the first locomotive and emu orders. Today all the earlier motive power has been converted with silicon rectifiers and silicon is used exclusively in new building. The mercury-arc traction rectifier was overshadowed by the new devices from the beginning. It was not really suited to mobile use in spite of the effort put into improving it and it had the drawback that it needed preheating before being put on load if stock was stored in the open in cold weather. Germanium, too, had a relatively short life. Overloads producing high temperature could cause a breakdown. Silicon was more tolerant in this respect and silicon rectifiers with power ratings suitable for traction became available sooner than had been foreseen.

In a steam locomotive most of the visible parts have something to do with its working. Little can be seen of the 'works' of an electric locomotive except the roof-mounted pantograph and circuit-breaker. The pictures on pages 22 and 23 of this collection of a 1,500V dc locomotive of Class 76 on a Woodhead route freight duty, and of Class 87s on the LMR 25kV ac electrification, give no hint that in less than 40 years the changes that have taken place are more fundamental than in the whole period of steam locomotive development.

Classes 81 to 85 were followed by another 100 locomotives of Class 86 of higher power (3,600/4,000hp) and modified in various ways on the basis of experience with their forerunners. Electric braking (rheostatic) was introduced and has been used again in the Class 87s built for extension of the West Coast Main Line electrification to Glasgow, but other 86 features were less successful. They were found to be hard on the track and have since either been restricted to 80mph or given a modified suspension system and wheels incorporating rubber between the tyre

and wheel centre to provide resilience. The modified suspension is on the Flexicoil system also used in Class 87 and easily recognised by the groups of vertical coil springs which support the locomotive body. As well as absorbing vertical shocks, the springs allow for the sideways movements between body and bogie which are otherwise permitted by a swing bolster. Class 87 is a 5,000hp locomotive still weighing only 80 tons. The class consists of 35 locomotives with an electro-mechanical control system similar to the preceding classes and one, 87.101, with thyristor control. A thyristor is a silicon rectifier which will both convert alternating to direct current and control the dc voltage. In 87.101 the driver can either operate his controller in the same way as if he was 'notching up' a locomotive with conventional electro-mechanical tap-changer control or he can preset a suitable tractive effort on a dial on his desk, when the locomotive will maintain that effort automatically throughout the period of acceleration, checking wheelslip if it occurs.

The next step in motive power for high-speed passenger service on the West Coast Main Line is the electric Advanced Passenger Train, which

*Above:* The 'Western Tribute' railtour waits to leave Plymouth North Road on 26 February 1977 for the run to Paddington which symbolised the end of the 'Western' class diesel-hydraulics on the Western Region. No 1023 *Western Fusilier* leads No 1013 *Western Ranger.* / M. Galvin

*Right:* On the Dart Valley Railway 0-4-2T *Ashburton* carries the Royal train headcode as it leaves Buckfastleigh for Totnes Riverside on Jubilee Day 7 June 1977. / *Peter Zabek*

began running trials in 1958. The basic power unit is a 4,000hp power car, one or two of which are marshalled in the middle of the train according to its length. As the train rounds curves, the vehicle bodies are automatically tilted inwards by up to 9° so that at 125mph the sideways force felt by passengers is no more than in a conventional train on the same curvature at 100mph. The APT traction motors are thyristor controlled. They are carried inside the power car body like the engine of a diesel locomotive and drive the axles through cardan shafts similar to those which transmitted the drive in diesel-hydraulic locomotives.

While all these developmens have been taking place the Southern Railway has continued with its long-established 750V dc electrification system,

14

but here too there were important innovations in the Bournemouth electrification of 1967. Previously the number of coaches propelled in a push-pull train had rarely exceeded two, but tests on the Southern showed that there could be as many as eight 'pushed from behind' even at speeds around 90mph. In the fast buffet car trains on the Bournemouth service a four-car set with two motorcoaches totalling 3,000hp leaves Waterloo propelling two four-car sets of trailers. From Bournemouth the leading four-car trailer set is taken on to Weymouth by a Class 33 diesel-electric locomotive. On the return trip the four-car set is propelled by the diesel from Weymouth to Bournemouth and attached without further shunting to the rear of the fast electric to Waterloo waiting in the station.

Another contribution of the Southern to modern railway operating is the development of dual-power units capable of working away from the live rail when necessary. They were first seen in the ten electric/battery motor luggage vans built for boat trains on the Kent Coast electrification in 1959, which travel from Victoria to Dover as ordinary motorcoaches, taking power from the live rail, and at Dover can operate on their batteries over the non-electrified quayside lines. In 1962 the first of the Class 73 electro-diesel locomotives appeared, equipped with a 1,600hp electric installation for use on live rail sections and an auxiliary 600hp diesel engine to provide power on non-electrified lines and in sidings. The electro-diesels can run in multiple with emu motorcoaches when necessary. In the early days of the Bournemouth electrification, when there was a shortage of rolling stock, they were often to be seen replacing one of the motorcoaches in the power section of a Bournemouth/Weymouth train. In these circumstances they can be controlled from an ordinary emu controller. The Region's Class 33 diesel-electrics are similarly versatile. There has been one working on a which train from Salisbury headed by a Class 33 has been combined at Basingstoke with an emu from Southampton. From Basingstoke to Waterloo the Class 33 heads the formation and its driver is in control both of the locomotive power plant and the traction equipments of the emu stock in the rear.

Since 1977 the suburban services at Kings Cross have been electrified and new generations of standard BR emu stock are coming into service. Class 312, based on the earlier 310 units built for Euston outer suburban services, has a top speed of 90mph in several of its versions and is gangwayed throughout each set. This type will be widely used for the longer-distance commuter services. Class 313 has been designed specifically for the Welwyn and Hertford to Moorgate service of the GN Suburban scheme, which changes at Drayton Park from the 25kV of the open air sections to 750V dc for the underground section to Moorgate. The Class 313 motorcoaches have a dc power circuit which is fed at a fixed voltage through rectifiers when running on 25kV. Underground, the rectifiers are bypassed and dc from the third rail is taken direct to the power circuits.

## Preservation Today

By the time steam traction ended on British Rail the Preservation movement was already flourishing. In the eyes of many of the general public at first it may have seemed a somewhat despairing gesture by enthusiasts determined to keep the past alive. But soon the fascination of the steam locomotive reasserted itself even in minds where it had lain dormant for many years. The lines began to attract the business that was necessary for their survival and gradually they moved into their present position as an accepted part of the 'leisure industry', winning invaluable support from the Tourist Boards. The Welsh Tourist Board made the narrow-gauge lines in Wales widely known by its *Great Little Trains of Wales* timetable and information folders, and tourist offices all over Britain now take care to be informed on the activities of preserved lines in their areas. In Peterborough the Nene Valley Railway is promoted by the Peterborough Development Corporation as one of the amenities of the Nene Park which has been planned as one of the attractions of the expanded city.

At first the preserved railways were generally self-contained, like the Festiniog, Talyllyn, and Welshpool & Llanfair; or reopened sections of closed secondary lines, like the Bluebell Railway. Now, however, there are stretches of main line among them. In Leicestershire part of the old Great Central main line to London Marylebone has been reopened by the Main Line Steam Trust between Loughborough and Rothley for operation by the Great Central Railway Co (1976) Ltd, bringing a great name as well as part of a great line back to life. In Devon the Dart Valley Railway operates the line from Paignton to Kingswear as the Torbay & Dartmouth Railway, the name by which it was known when opened in 1864. There are cross-platform connections with Western Region main-line trains at Paignton, carrying on a service once provided by through coaches from Paddington to Kingswear (for Dartmouth).

Yorkshire, where the Keighley & Worth Valley, North Yorkshire Moors and Yorkshire Dales lines have long been resorts for the enthusiast, gained a new steam-worked passenger line in 1977 when the Lord Mayor of York inaugurated a passenger service on the Derwent Valley Railway between Layerthorpe Station (York) and Dunnington. The Derwent Valley, an industrial railway which had not worked regular passenger trains since 1926, had experimented with enthusiasts' steam specials a year earlier, the trains being hauled by the ex-LNWR 2-4-0 *Hardwicke* loaned from the National Railway Museum. They were so popular that the railway bought its own steam tank engine, an ex-NER 0-6-0, and attached passenger coaches to certain trains serving the Dunnington Industrial Estate, often coupled to grain wagons conveying grain from a drying plant at Dunnington. At Layerthorpe the wagons are shunted into exchange sidings and forwarded to their destinations by British Rail. Other freight trains on the line are worked by Drewry diesel locomotives.

The preserved lines are no longer only concerned with enthusiast or tourist patronage. They often aim at providing a transport service for residents along their routes who have been deprived of a railway service since the line was closed by British Rail. Sometimes it is planned to run diesel railcars throughout the year and steam trains at holiday periods. The West Somerset is one of the lines where this type of operation is important.

Another preservation activity is the steam centre, usually with lengths of track on which rides can be given behind steam locomotives. Typical examples are Didcot with its all-Great Western atmosphere, the Midland Railway Centre at Butterley, Derbyshire, and Carnforth, where the fleet of famous main-line locomotives includes a Pacific of the Northern Railway of France.

Only a handful of all the lines now operating can be mentioned here. Not only do they keep steam alive but today some of them are homes for diesels which have been retired from BR by the pressure of advancing technology. As HSTs and APTs increasingly dominate the British Rail scene it is comforting to know that old friends are still intact on the preserved lines and at the preservation movement's centres. If you have time for nothing else when you are in York, at least take a bus to Layerthorpe and see the jet of steam from a safety valve rising above the factory roofs. Time really does run backwards then.

*B. K. Cooper*

*Below:* Snowdon Mountain Railway 0-4-2T No 4 *Snowdon* propels a train over Afon Hwch Viaduct as it leaves Llanberis for the Summit. / *Allan Stewart*

# STEAM FINALE

*Above:* Dirty smoke swirls from Stanier 'Black Five' No 45212 as it passes Shap Summit with a Glasgow-Morecambe express in April 1964. / *Derek Cross*

*Below:* A northbound freight from Carlisle crosses the River Clyde near Crawford on the Caledonian main line behind a 'Black Five' No 45259 in March 1964. / *Derek Cross*

*Above right:* BR Standard Class 9F 2-10-0 No 92223 draws a Long Meg-Widnes anhydrite train across Ais Gill Viaduct in the beautiful Mallerstang Valley in February 1964. / *Derek Cross*

*Below right:* In the typical dirty condition of the 'Britannia' Pacifics in their later days, No 70039, *Sir Christopher Wren* climbs Shap with a train formed entirely of ex-LMS stock in September 1964. / *Derek Cross*

*Above:* Stanier 'Duchess' Pacific No 46225 *Duchess of Gloucester* appears to be making light work climbing Shap at the head of a Euston-Carlisle train in June 1962. / *Noel A. Machell*

*Below:* Great Western 'County' class No 1011 *County of Chester* passes a permanent way gang in Sonning Cutting with an unidentified up train carrying express headlamps in the summer of 1960. / *Derek Cross*

*Right:* Constructed in 1950, No 7029 *Clun Castle* was among the last of the classic line of GWR four-cylinder 4-6-0s. Directly descended from G. J. Churchward's *North Star* of 1906, No 7029 is seen here at Princes Risborough in June 1964 heading the last scheduled steam passenger train from Paddington, the 16.15 to Banbury. / *G. S. Cocks*

One of Britain's most numerous and longest-lived mixed traffic 4-6-0s was the GWR 'Hall' class. *Below:* No 6960 *Raveningham Hall* pulls out of Oxford with a through train to Bournemouth in October 1963. / *Ivo Peters*

*Below right:* Recalling the locomotive exchange of 1925 'Castle' class No 7029 *Clun Castle* leaves Kings Cross with an Ian Allan special to Leeds in September 1967. / *Brian Stephenson*

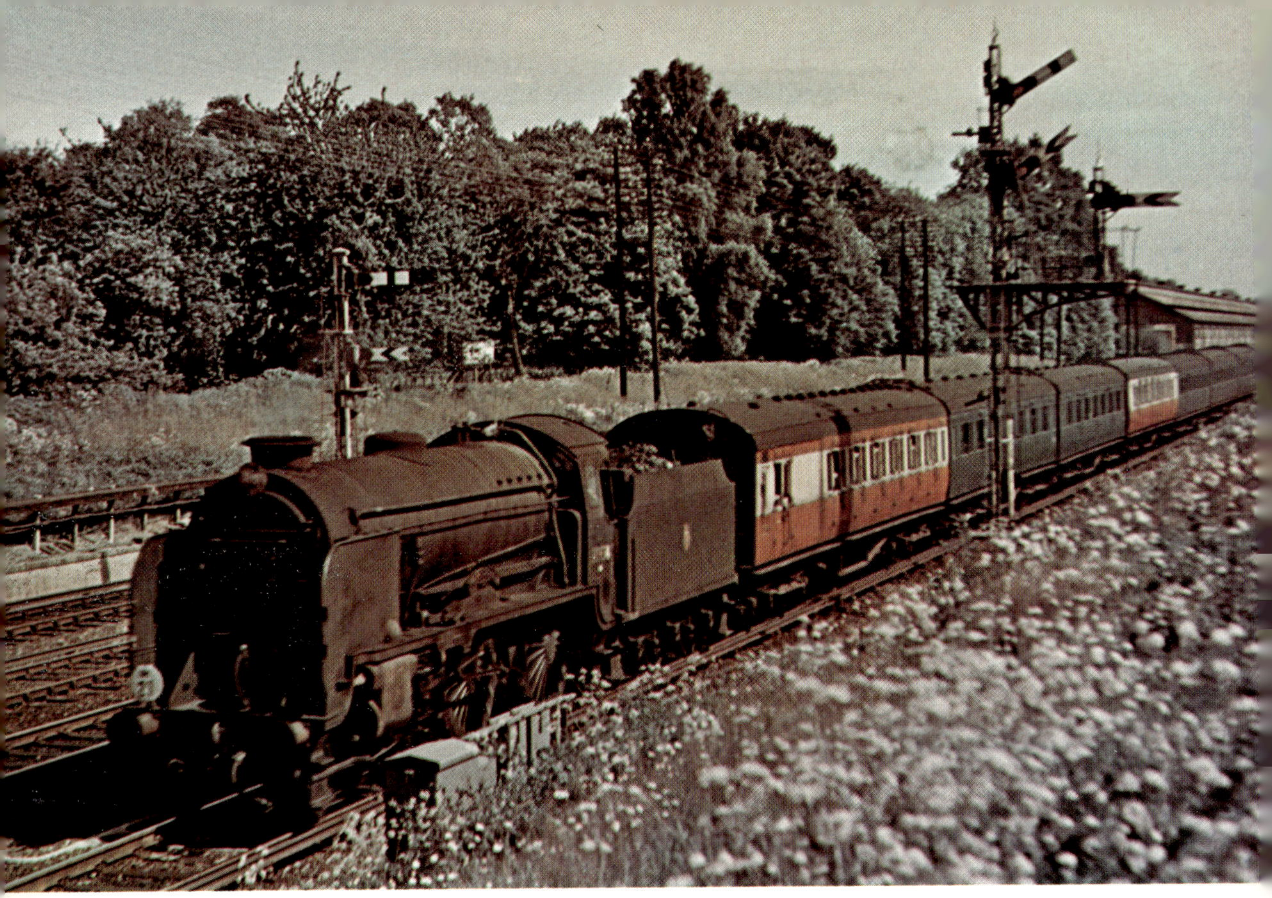

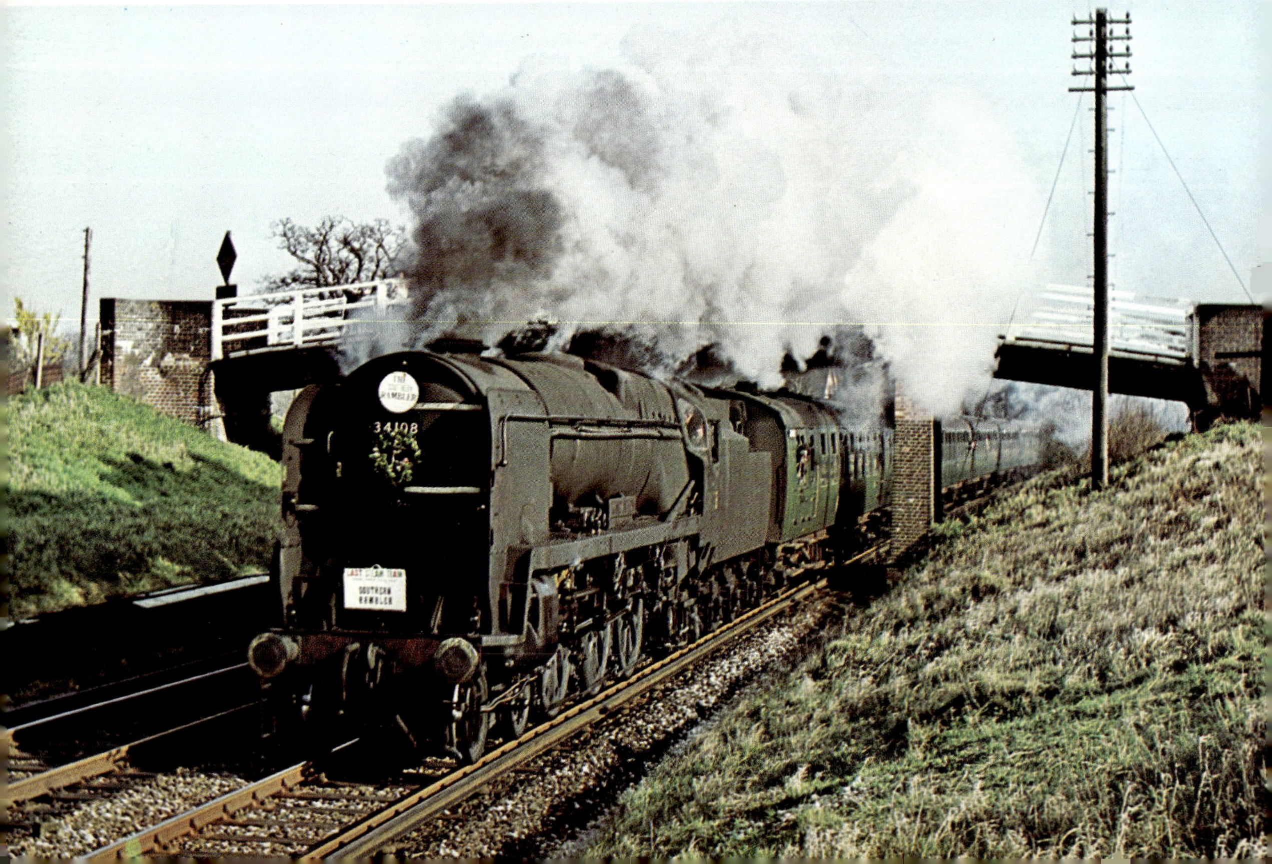
34108
SOUTHERN
RAMBLER

*Left:* BR plum and spilt milk mingles with Southern green behind 'Schools' class No 30924 *Haileybury* forming a Dover-London train passing Orpington in July 1960. / *Derek Cross*

*Below left:* Modified Bulleid 'West Country' class Pacific No 34108 *Wincanton* nears Plumpton with a special train returning from Eastbourne to Victoria. / *Brian Stephenson*

*Below:* Maunsell 'King Arthur' class N15 No 30806 *Sir Galleron* makes an all-out effort on restarting a Victoria-Ramsgate express from Bromley South in May 1959. / *Derek Cross*

*Above:* Bulleid 'West Country' class No 34023 *Blackmore Vale* arrives at Wareham with the LCGB 'Dorset Coast Express' from Waterloo in May 1967. This engine is now preserved on the Bluebell Railway / *Brian Stephenson*

*Above right:* 'Schools' class No 30911 *Dover* pulls away from Merstham with a London Bridge-Reading and Tonbridge train in May 1962. / *G. D. King*

*Right:* 'Merchant Navy' class No 35001 *Channel Packet* accelerates through Shorncliffe with an up boat train for Victoria in 1959.

30911

SHORNCLIFFE
35001
H

WATERLOO

*Above:* 'West Country' class No 34037 *Clovelly* takes the last steam-hauled passenger service out of Waterloo, a boat train to Southampton Docks, at 18.20 on 8 July 1967. / *Klaus Marx*

*Below:* Peppercorn Class K1 No 62045 is seen near Billingham at the head of a Ferryhill-West Hartlepool dolomite ore train in June 1967. / *John M. Boyes*

*Top left:* With a set of chocolate and cream Pullman cars forming the up 'Yorkshire Pullman' Class A1 No 60141 *Abbotsford* nears London at Potters Bar in September 1961. / *J. W. Millbank*

*Left:* Class V2 No 60970 restarts an Aberdeen-Glasgow express away from Gleneagles in September 1963. / *Derek Cross*

*Above:* In the last two weeks of steam Raven NER Class Q6 No 63395 crosses the River Wear from Monkswearmouth to Sunderland with a Hylton Colliery to Sunderland Docks coal train in August 1967. / *Brian Stephenson*

31

# BRITISH RAIL ROVER
## North & East

*Left:* Class 47 No 47.408, skirts the sea near Lamberton Beach on the East Coast main line with a southbound express in June 1976. / *L. A. Nixon*

*Below left:* A Newcastle-Liverpool train travels south past Newsham on the East Coast main line north of Thirsk in June 1975 headed by Class 46 No 46.040. / *L. Riley*

*Below:* At Mistley station in June 1974 a Harwich-Liverpool Street train headed by a Class 37 locomotive meets another Class 37-hauled train from Ipswich. / *G. R. Mortimer*

*Above:* Class 55 'Deltic' 3,300hp diesel-electric No 9019 *Royal Highland Fusilier* climbs past Belle Isle on the exit from Kings Cross with a down express. / *Brian Stephenson*

*Right:* Class 45 No 45.013 heads the Edinburgh-Plymouth train past Grantshouse on the East Coast main line in September 1976. / *Mrs D. A. Robinson*

GRANTSHOUSE

# Midland

*Above:* Class 76 1,500 dc Bo-Bo No 76.055 heads an eastbound freight near Woodhead on the ex-GC Manchester-Sheffield line in September 1976. / *Mrs D. A. Robinson*

*Below:* Class 87 No 87.034 on a Birmingham-Glasgow train is seen at Shap Wells in August 1976. / *Mrs D. A. Robinson*

*Right:* On the West Coast main line a London-bound train from Birmingham emerges from Kilsby Tunnel south of Rugby. The locomotive is No 87.020. / *J. H. Cooper-Smith*

*Right:* Class 81 No 81.005 passes Salop Goods Junction, Crewe, with a BOC block train from Wolverhampton to Widnes. / *David M. Cross*

*Below:* A pair of Class 50s, Nos 401 and 403 (50.001 and 50.003) head the up 'Royal Scot' at Carronbridge in 1971. / *Derek Cross*

*Below right:* A train of assorted passenger stock is taken through the Lune Gorge by English Electric Type 4 No D200 (now 40.122) in the early 1960s.

8Z76

1S28

*Left:* On the Settle-Carlisle line a brace of Class 31s head north from Skipton with a mixed freight in July 1971. / *J. Winkley*

*Below left:* Class 47 No 1721 (47.130) is seen near Helwith Bridge with a Leeds-Glasgow relief train in September 1973. / *Derek Cross*

*Right:* A northbound mineral train with No 25.236 in charge is seen leaving Blea Moor Tunnel in June 1975. / *J. H. Cooper Smith*

*Below:* A Class 40 heads a train of tank wagons across Dandry Mire Viaduct. / *J. Winkley*

# Freedom of Scotland

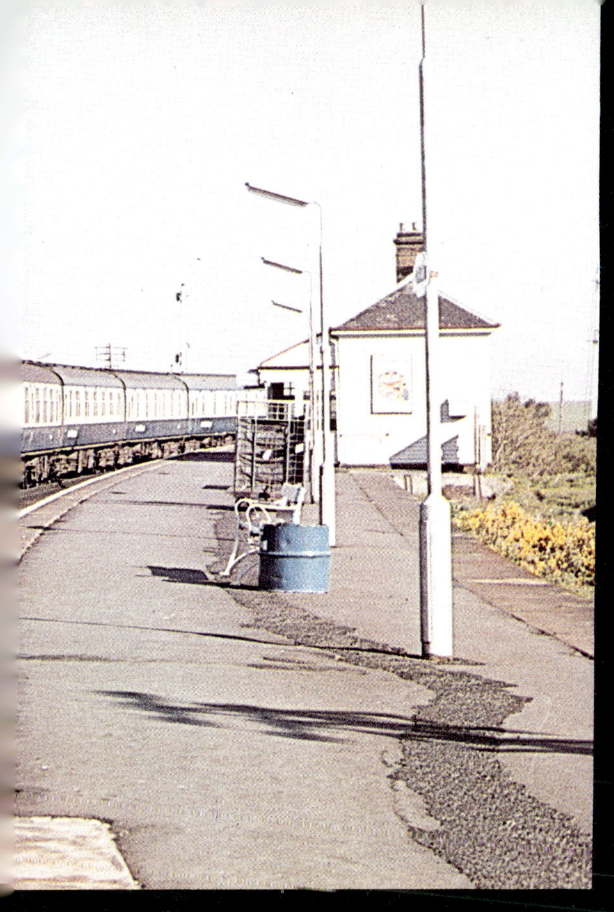

*Left:* Class 50 No 50.021 arrives with a special train at Girvan on the line from Glasgow to Stranraer. / *Derek Cross*

*Below left:* Class 24 No 24.119 heads a Wick-Inverness train at Dingwall in August 1975. / *L. Riley*

*Below:* A Dundee-Edinburgh dmu approaches Markinch in April 1977. / *S. Mairs*

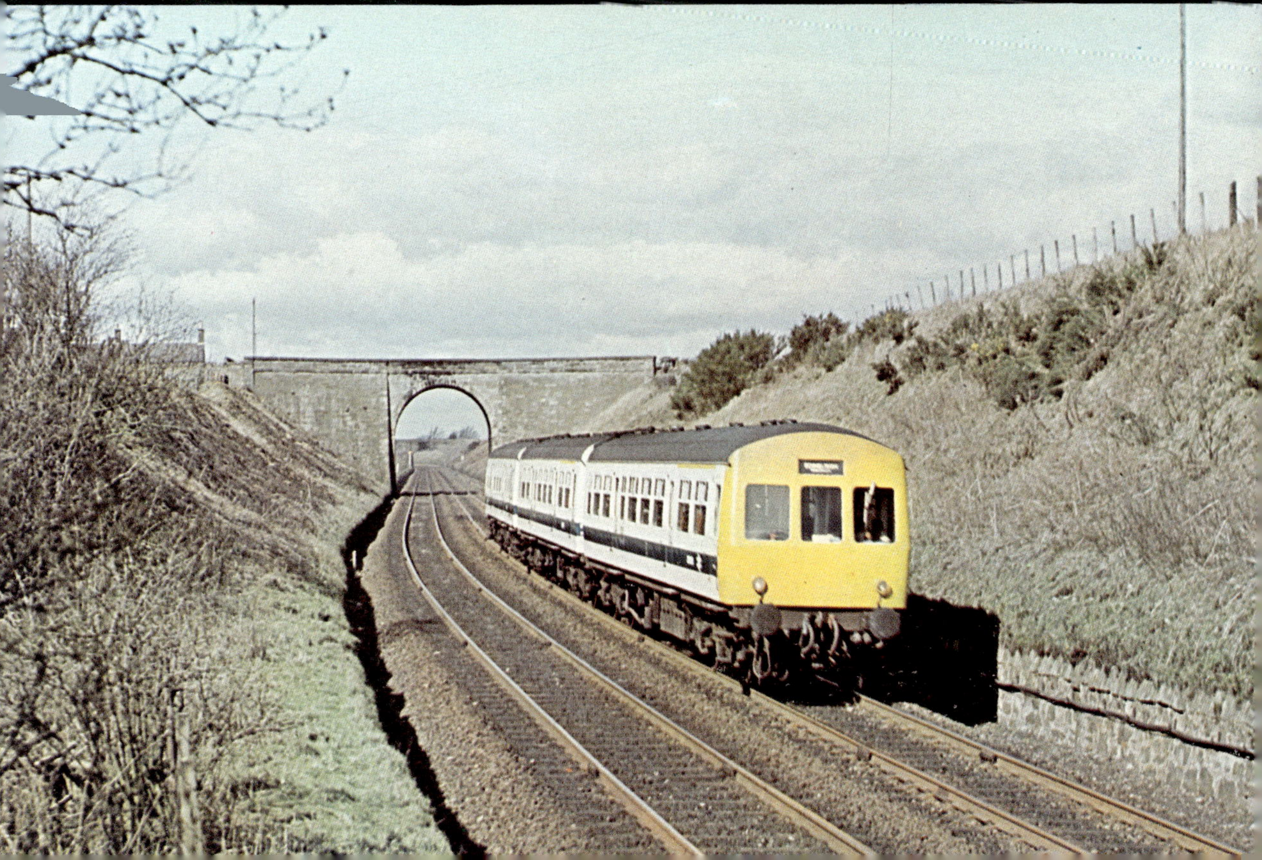

*Above left:* A Dundee-Glasgow train headed by Class 27 No 27.032 is seen near Stirling in May 1976. / *Peter J. Robinson*

*Above:* Class 26/1 No 5330 (now 26.030) and Class 24/1 No 5126 (now 24.126) approach Aviemore station with the 16.35 Inverness-Glasgow train. / *N. E. Preedy*

*Left:* Two Class 24s, Nos 5115 (24.115) and 5132 (24.132) head a Bristol-Kyle of Lochalsh excursion over the Kyle line at Attadale in September 1973. /*Derek Cross*

# South & West

*Right:* Class 47 No D1712 (47.123) heads a Bournemouth-Waterloo train of assorted liveries in the New Forest near Brockenhurst a few weeks before electrification in 1967.
/ *Derek Cross*

*Below:* A train from Waterloo enters the Eastleigh complex in May 1976. / *Brian Morrison*

*Below right:* A boat train leaves Folkestone Harbour for Victoria with a motor luggage van bringing up the rear. / *M. Pudduck*

Exeter St Davids

*Left:* Leaving the Exe Estuary behind, Class 47 No 47.524 gives passengers on a Cardiff-Penzance train a glimpse of open sea as a foretaste of what is to come on emerging from the short cutting at Dawlish Warren. / *L. Riley*

*Below left:* A Waterloo-Exeter train arrives at Exeter St Davids behind Class 33 No 6528 (33.111) in August 1975. / *Norman E. Preedy*

*Below:* Class 50 No 50.046 passes Newton Abbot with the Sunday down 'Cornish Riviera Limited' in September 1976. / *L. Riley*

*Above:* Multiple working on the Western Region, Class 31s Nos 31.259 and 31.258 head a Paddington-Oxford train at Twyford in June 1975. / *D. Moulden*

*Below:* A rake of 10 preserved GWR coaches form a Bridgnorth (SVR) to Paddington special. 'The Severn Valley Limited' is here seen in care of No 47.120 approaching Middle Hill Tunnel at Box. / *Ivo Peters*

*Right:* 'Western' Class 52 No 1073 *Western Bulwark* heads an up train through Sonning Cutting in 1972. / *J. H. Cooper-Smith*

*Below right:* A Liskeard to Looe train formed of a single-car dmu pauses at Sandplace to pick up its solitary passenger. / *L. Tindall*

# Inter-City 125



*Below:* Class 253 HST unit No 253.006 emerges from Middle Hill Tunnel, at Box, in September 1976. / *Ivo Peters*

*Right:* No 253.004 leaves Newport Tunnel on a down crew training run to Swansea in August 1976. / *Ivo Peters*

253004

# PRESERVATION TODAY 1    Welsh narrow gauge

*Above:* BR's only steam-operated line is the Vale of Rheidol Railway from Aberystwyth to Devil's Bridge. Here No 8 *Llywelyn* crosses the River Rheidol in June 1976. / *John Scrace*

*Below:* On the Festiniog Railway No 2 *Prince* waits to leave Portmadoc (now Porthmadog) with a train for Tan-y-Bwlch. / *S. W. Stevens-Stratten*

*Above:* On the Llanberis Lake Railway No 3 *Dolbadarn* calls at Cel Llydan with a train from Penllyn to Gilfach Ddu in 1976. / *N. J. Hayllar*

*Below:* No 2 *Dolgoch* crosses Dolgoch Viaduct with a Tywyn-Abergynolwyn train on the Talyllyn Railway in August 1973. / *John Scrace*

# PRESERVATION TODAY 2
## Standard gauge

*Below:* L&SWR Class 415 4-4-2T No 488 is seen here working on the Bluebell Railway in 1974, Britain's first preserved standard gauge line. / *Allan Stewart*

*Right:* A GWR Churchward 2-6-2T No 4588 guides a Kingswear-Paignton train round Noss Curve on the Torbay & Dartmouth Railway in 1976. / *L. A. Nixon*

*Below right:* Class 4MT No 43106 leaves Bridgnorth on the Severn Valley Railway in April 1976. / *D. H. Ballantyne*

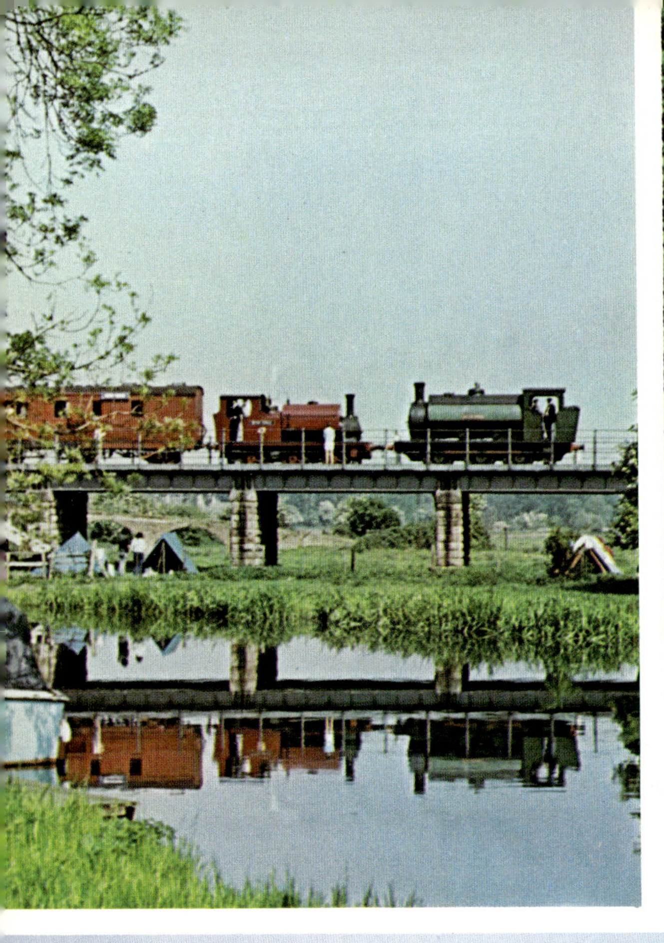

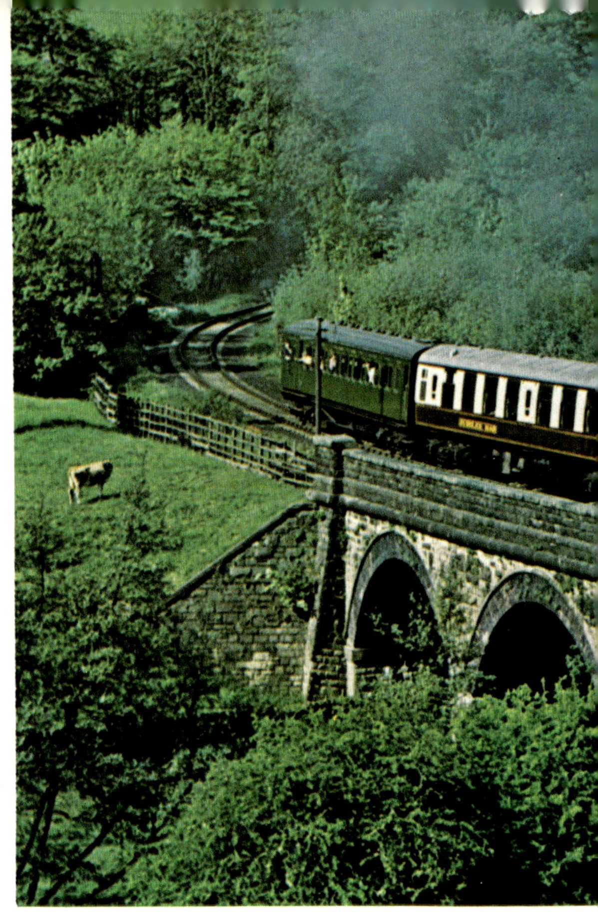

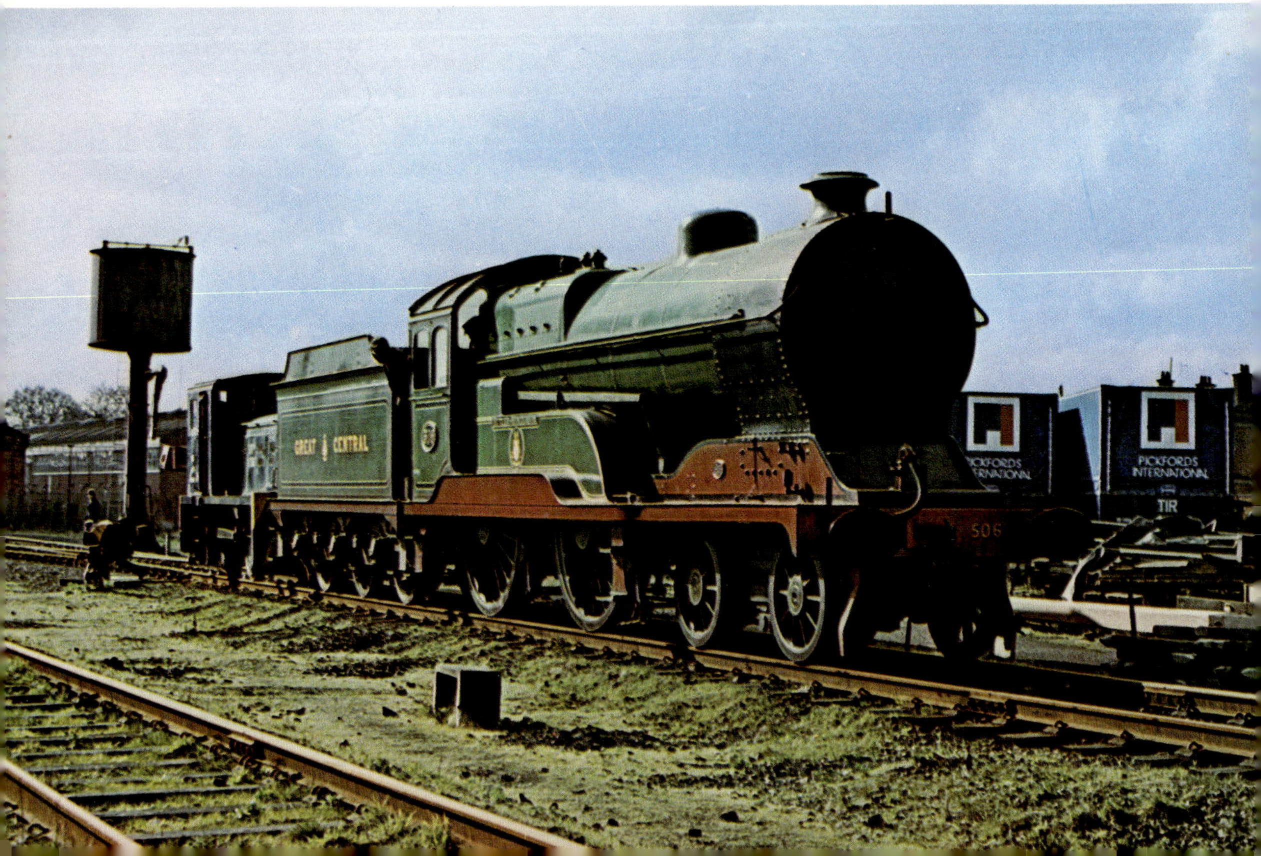
GREAT CENTRAL
PICKFORDS
INTERNATIONAL
TIR
506

*Above left:* Hunslet 0-6-0 No 1953 *Jacks Green* and Hudswell Clarke 0-6-0ST No 1539 *Derek Crouch* are reflected in a tranquil River Nene as they pause during shunting operations at Wansford, on the Nene Valley Railway. / *Brian Sharpe*

*Above:* On loan from the National Railway Museum collection GNR 4-4-2 No 990 heads a Pullman special over Mytholmes Viaduct on the Keighley and Worth Valley Railway in June 1977. / *Nigel Trotter*

*Left:* Also on loan from the NRM, former Great Central 'Director' class 4-4-0 No 506 *Butler-Henderson* is now preserved at Loughborough. / *J. H. Cooper-Smith*

*Right:* On the Torbay & Dartmouth Railway a train leaves Churston for Paignton hauled by GWR 64xx class 0-6-0T No 6412 in May 1975. / *Patrick Russell*

*Above:* Ex-Lambton Colliery 0-6-2T No 29 heads a Grosmont-Goathland train at Beck Holes on the North Yorkshire Moors Railway in July 1976. / *Mrs D. A. Robinson*

*Left:* Stanier 'Black Five' No 5212, now preserved on the Keighley & Worth Valley Railway is seen with a Keighley-Oxenhope train in August 1969. / *Brian Stephenson*

*Right:* Class K1 No 2005 leaves Grosmont for Goathland on the North Yorkshire Moors Railway in October 1976. / *Mrs D. A. Robinson*

45110

*Above:* Stanier 'Black Five' No 45110 *RAF Biggin Hill* skirts Trimpley Reservoir on the Severn Valley Railway in May 1976 with a typical train of the 1950s. / *D. C. Williams*

*Below:* One of two preserved Class 9Fs, No 92203 *Black Prince*, owned by David Shepherd, and normally on display at Cranmore, in Somerset, is here seen approaching Romsey with a special train in April 1975. / *M. Ravensdale*

The 'Gainsborough Model Railway Society Special' train from York to Carnforth crosses Knaresborough Viaduct in April 1976, motive power supplied by a London & North Western Railway 2-4-0 No 790, *Hardwicke* built in 1873 and a Midland Railway Compound 4-4-0 No 1000 built in 1902. Both locomotives were provided by the National Railway Museum. / *Allan Stewart*